Lunch
välkomna
Tomatsoppa
bröd
kaffe o kaka
100 kr
välkomna
Mors
godaste
sylt
kaka
Lunch
Tomatsoppa med
Bondomelett
välkomna

Kakao förlag
Box 1505
221 01 Lund

ISBN 9789187795138

Recipes, text and styling: Milo Kalén
Photographs and styling: Tine Guth Linse
Graphic design: Edholm & Ullenius
Repro: Italgraf Media
Printing in Estonia
via Italgraf Media, 2016

Swedish FIKA

FROM DELI SANDWICHES
TO CAKES AND COFFEE

tuvwx
6789
EFGH

Kak
på
Kak

A dream come true!

I'd just turned 51 and felt it was my time now. I wanted to realise my dream and open a café where I'd bake just like you do at home - with an open kitchen. I've always loved going into pizzerias where you can see the pizza master at work and can stand and point to the ingredients you want. I wanted that kind of feel!

The three words that guided my search for the perfect premises were warmth, feeling and experience. Finally, I found it, just a few hundred metres from where we live, a bit hidden and tucked away but still in the centre of Limhamn. This was where I was going to open my café! So we got to work. Walls and ceilings were torn down, new tiles and furnishings went up. And I built a kitchen that was fully visible from the café.

My passion for cooking and baking is something I inherited from my mother. She was a pro at making the 'seven types of cake and cookies' that are essential for a traditional Swedish fika. And we had lots of fika! Sewing bees, coffee parties, morning coffee, afternoon coffee, evening fika - there was always an occasion to enjoy her fabulous home baking. I didn't do that much baking while I was young and still living at home; it was only after starting my own family that my interest awakened. And you should have seen how much ended up in the bin at first! Everything I made was rock hard and totally inedible! But perseverance paid off, and as my children and their circle of friends grew, so did my fika baking expertise.

In March 2013 it was time to open my very own café! With the sweet smell of buns in the oven and a little help from Facebook and Instagram, the guests started dropping in...

When I'm in the kitchen...

Flavour comes first,
good ingredients second,
and it has to be fuss-free!

Something I often say when I'm explaining how to make a cake, soup or bake bread is: "Don't worry about it too much." And you really don't have to - as long as you're enjoying what you're doing. Taste it, feel the consistency, use the ingredients you like, and it'll be great! Be adventurous too. If it fails, well, OK - sometimes you have to throw it away and start again. Then, once you've got the knack - experiment! Knead your dough for a longer or shorter time, make different shapes or add delicious fillings. Try substituting part of the flour with another kind; brush and decorate your pastries with different things. It's about finding your favourites. I love vanilla, which I'm sure you'll notice from the recipes. If it says a teaspoon, I use at least a tablespoon. And rosemary - that must be God's gift to humanity!

I hope this book inspires you to try my favourite recipes and create your own. Play with the recipes - add a pinch of salt or sugar, even if it doesn't say so. Or tip the dough onto an oven tray instead of into a baking tin. Have fun and get stuck in!

Milo

kaka
kaka
Appelmust
small but mighty
froosh
CITRON

SHORTCRUST PASTRY

Basic cookie dough

This is a basic dough from which you can make all kinds of different cookies. Here you can see jam thumbprints, currant cookies, Brussels cookies and Mazarins but you can shape them any way you like and add all sorts of fillings. It's the perfect dough to experiment with!

250 g butter left out of the fridge
for approx. ½ hour

400 ml flour
125 ml potato flour
just under 200 ml sugar
½ tsp. baking powder

Put all the ingredients in your Kitchen-Aid bowl or food processor and mix until the dough starts to clump together. You can also mix the dough by hand. Scoop the mixture out onto a pastry board or work surface and knead briskly to form a dough. Leave the dough to rest for about 30 minutes in a cool place (but preferably not in the fridge, which is a little too cold!). Your basic dough is now ready.

Let your imagination run wild!

Once you've made the basic dough, you can roll it however you like and use your favourite flavourings and fillings. Good luck!

Milo fingers
Fork cookies

Jam thumbprints
Brussels cookies

JAM
thumbprints

Makes approx. 50

1 quantity short crust pastry,
see page 12

100 ml raspberry jam

Set the oven to 175 °C (fan-assisted), otherwise 200 °C. Make the short crust pastry according to the recipe on page 12 and roll the dough into balls, approximately 3 cm in diameter. Put them on an oven tray lined with baking paper. Make a well in the centre of each ball with your thumb but don't press right through the dough or the jam will run out onto the oven tray. Spoon raspberry jam into the wells and bake the cookies in the centre of the oven for approximately 12 minutes.

Two types of
BRUSSELS COOKIE

One with cocoa...

Makes approx. 50

1 quantity short crust pastry, see page 12

approx. 2 tbsp. cocoa
200 ml pearl sugar
a few drops of red food colouring
1 beaten egg

Make the short crust pastry according to the recipe on page 12 and add the cocoa along with the other dry ingredients. Roll the dough into a log, approximately 5 cm in diameter. If you prefer, flatten it a little to make rectangular cookies, like in the picture. Leave the dough to rest in the refrigerator for at least half an hour. Tint the pearl sugar as described below.

Set the oven to 175 °C (fan-assisted), otherwise 200 °C. Take the dough log out of the fridge and brush with egg. Pour the coloured sugar onto a sheet of baking paper and roll the log in it. Cut into centimetre-thick slices and place on an oven tray lined with baking paper. Bake the cookies in the centre of the oven for approximately 10 minutes.

... and one without

Makes approx. 50

1 quantity short crust pastry, see page 12

approx. 200 ml caster sugar
a few drops of red food colouring
1 beaten egg

Make the short crust pastry according to the recipe on page 12. Roll the dough into a log measuring approximately 5 cm in diameter and store in the refrigerator for at least half an hour. Tint the caster sugar with the food colouring (see below).

Set the oven to 175 °C (fan-assisted), otherwise 200 °C. Take the log of dough out of the fridge and brush with the egg. Pour out the coloured sugar onto a sheet of baking paper and roll the log of dough in it. Cut into centimetre-thick slices and place on an oven tray lined with baking paper. Bake at the centre of the oven for approximately 10 minutes.

Tinted sugar

Pour a few drops of food colouring onto a dish and add the sugar. Stir it around with your fingers for a while and voilà, pretty tinted sugar!

Fork cookies

Makes approx. 50

1 quantity short crust pastry, see page 12
200 ml raisins

Set the oven to 175 °C (fan-assisted), otherwise 200 °C. Chop the raisins and make the short crust pastry according to the recipe on page 12 but also mix the raisins into the dough. Roll the dough into balls approximately 3 cm in diameter and put them on an oven tray lined with baking paper. Flatten the balls with a fork, leaving a striped impression, before baking in the centre of the oven for approximately 12 minutes.

Milo FINGERS

This recipe is a simplified version of Milan fingers and a favourite at the café.

Makes approx. 40

1 quantity short crust pastry, see page 12

1 beaten egg
a few drops of red food colouring
approx. 200 g almond paste
approx. 150 ml pearl sugar
100 ml flaked almonds

Set the oven to 175 °C (fan-assisted), otherwise 200 °C. Make the short crust pastry according to the recipe on page 12 and roll it out into a rectangle measuring approximately 10-15 cm wide and ½ cm thick. Brush with egg. Knead the food colouring into the almond paste and form a baton as thick as your forefinger and as long as the dough you have rolled out. Place the baton of almond paste along the bottom edge of the dough and roll up lengthways to encase the almond paste. Press the edges of the dough together and brush with beaten egg. Sprinkle pearl sugar and flaked almonds onto a sheet of baking paper and roll the dough in the mixture. Cut the dough into pieces - about 4-5 cm long is about right, I think. Place on an oven tray lined with baking paper and bake in the centre of the oven until golden brown (approximately 12 minutes).

matiga

WRINKLIES

or

jitterbugs

In Sweden, these cookies are usually known as jitterbugs but my mum used to call them 'wrinklies'. The number of times I've heard guests at the café sigh and say, "These are so hard to make!" But they're not. The problem might have something to do with being too careful. The dough is quite messy but no matter how 'ugly' the cookies look on the tray, they sort themselves out in the oven and come out all wonderfully wrinkly!

Makes approx. 40

1 quantity short crust pastry, see page 12

1 egg white
just under 100 ml caster sugar

Set the oven to 175 °C (fan-assisted), otherwise 200 °C. Make the short crust pastry according to the recipe on page 12 and roll it out into a rectangle measuring approximately 20 cm wide and ½ cm thick. Whisk the egg white until stiff and slowly pour in the sugar while you continue to whisk. Spread the meringue mixture thickly over the entire rectangle of dough. Use a spatula to help you fold in one of the long sides, rolling up the dough like a Swiss roll. Cut the roll into 2-3 cm thick slices and place cut side up on an oven tray lined with baking paper. Bake in the centre of the oven until golden, for approximately 10 minutes.

Have a nice sit down...

The oven is yawning with a smile
- it's been awake a long time, checking out the scene:
Kneading and baking to the heat of the hob
and the clang of the kitchen;
To the beat of the sputtering coffee machine.

Soon all the ingredients will have fallen into place,
Waiting to be tasted when the door opens,
When the first footsteps arrive.

They keep coming in; cups and plates descending on
tables, coffee-thirsty thoughts keep opening the door
And the clock keeps ticking happily:
just a drop more, please!

At noon, lunch time hunger sets in
Then a potpourri of everything and everyone, sitting,
laughing and smiling;
An extra bit of cheese with that slice of bread,
A nice cookie taken by the hand
And the piece of pie that speedily needs to occupy a
ravenous thought.

At last, four o'clock and the door shuts goodbye
Only to open tomorrow with freshly baked warmth
And the promise of another delicious day!

Stellan Hökfelt

Mazarin cake

1 quantity short crust pastry, see page 12

100-200 ml raspberry jam
125 g grated almonds
75 g softened butter
2 eggs
150 ml sugar

Glaze

300-400 ml icing sugar
a dollop of raspberry jam
a few drops of water

Set the oven to 180 °C (fan-assisted), otherwise 205 °C. Stick a sheet of baking paper to the bottom of a spring form - you don't need to grease the sides. Press the dough into the tin, allowing it to reach approximately 3 cm up the sides. Spread raspberry jam over the bottom. Grate the almonds in a nut grinder. Mix the butter, grated almonds, sugar and eggs in a mixing bowl and spoon the mixture over the bottom, carefully distributing it over the raspberry jam. Bake in the centre of the oven for approximately 30 minutes. Let the cake cool before prising it out of the tin. Pour the icing sugar into a mixing bowl and mix with the raspberry jam to make a pale pink glaze. If it gets too dry, add a few drops of water, but it should be thick when it's ready. Pour the glaze over the cake and spread carefully with a spatula. Serve with a dollop of lightly whipped cream.

Psst!

Look out for a nut grinder the next time you're at a flea market. They are indispensible for cookie baking!

God Jul

Instead *of* GINGER SNAPS...

Swedish pepparkakor (ginger snaps) should be super thin, but I don't really have the patience for that so I usually make these instead. They're delicious and extremely easy!

Makes approx. 40

100 g softened butter
100 ml sugar
50 ml pale syrup
1 tsp. ground cinnamon
1 tsp. ground ginger
½ tsp. ground cloves
100 g flaked almonds
approx. 300 ml flour
½ tsp. bicarbonate of soda

Put butter, sugar and syrup in a bowl and use an electric whisk to beat until fluffy. Mix the spices, almonds, flour and bicarbonate of soda in another bowl and then stir into the mixture.

Whisk again to form a crumble and then press the dough together with your hands. Tip the dough onto a floured surface and make a roll, approximately 4 cm in diameter. Flatten the roll to make it rectangular and wrap in cling film before leaving to chill in the refrigerator for at least 4 hours. Heat the oven to 175 °C (fan-assisted), otherwise 200 °C. Take out the dough and cut it into thin slices with a really sharp knife.

Put the slices on an oven tray lined with baking paper and bake at the centre of the oven for 10-12 minutes. Allow the ginger snaps to cool before storing in a jar.

Psst!

The old 'coffee cup' measure is roughly 150 ml.

Grandma's cookies or Swedish BISCOTTI

My grandma used to bake these little rusks, and then my mother after her. It was also the thing that got me liking coffee. I would sit on Grandma's lap and dip the rusk in her coffee... a fond childhood memory.

Makes approx. 40

150 g softened butter
1 coffee cup of caster sugar
1 heaped coffee cup of grated almonds
1 egg
3 ½ coffee cups of flour
1 tsp. baking powder

Garnish

1 beaten egg
2 tbsp. caster sugar
2 tbsp. grated almonds

Set the oven to 175 °C (fan-assisted), otherwise 200 °C. Grate the almonds in a nut grinder. Quickly whisk all the ingredients together in a mixing bowl. Scoop the dough out onto your work surface and shape into three long rolls, each measuring approximately 4 cm in diameter. Put the rolls on an oven tray lined with baking paper and flatten them a little. Brush with the beaten egg before mixing the sugar and grated almonds and sprinkling over the rolls. Bake in the centre of the oven until golden brown (approximately 15 minutes). Remove the rolls and reduce the oven temperature to 75 °C (fan-assisted), otherwise 100 °C. Cut the rolls diagonally into pieces that are approximately 2 cm wide and arrange on the oven tray cut-side up, leaving them to dry in the oven for at least 1 hour. Store the rusks in an airtight jar. Best enjoyed dipped in hot black coffee!

Fina's
SYRUP SLICES

I got this recipe from my best friend, Fina. When my kids were small, my own recipe for these cookies just wasn't good enough – it had to be Fina's! The number you make depends on how large you cut them.

Makes approx. 40

200 g butter (not straight from the fridge)
175 ml sugar
1 tbsp. pale syrup (or golden syrup)
2 tbsp. vanilla sugar
500 ml flour
2 tsp. baking powder

Set the oven to 175 °C (fan-assisted), otherwise 200 °C. Cut the butter into small pieces. Mix everything together as far as possible in a bowl before scooping the dough out onto a pastry board or your work surface. Knead it together with your hands. Divide the dough into three pieces and roll them out to fit the length of your oven tray. Arrange the dough rolls on the tray (lined with baking paper) and flatten. Bake at the centre of the oven for approximately 15 minutes.

Take out the oven tray and diagonally cut the cookie lengths while still warm. Allow to cool before removing from the oven tray.

Oat lace COOKIES

These crispy little, leaf-thin lace cookies are something I often rustle up when I realise I've forgotten to make dessert. Served with vanilla ice-cream and warm berry compote, they're a luxurious treat!

Makes approx. 15

75 g melted butter
100 ml sugar
100 ml rolled oats
100 ml all-purpose flour
¼ tsp. baking powder
¼ dl milk
¼ dl pale syrup

Set the oven to 175 °C (fan-assisted), otherwise 200 °C. Melt the butter. Mix the sugar, rolled oats, all-purpose flour and baking powder in a mixing bowl. Add the milk, syrup and the melted butter. Quickly mix together and use a teaspoon to spoon out onto an oven tray lined with baking paper. Leave some space between each cookie because the mixture will spread out quite a lot. Bake at the centre of the oven until golden brown, for about 10-15 minutes. Allow to cool before removing from the oven tray.

50 kr
60 kr
Mighty Leaf
kaka

vild med salater
LOUISA LORANG
kaka kaka
Lunch
TISD. morotssoppa med topping
ONSD. paj m. salami mm
TORSD. risotto m. räkor
FRED. stuffade paprikor på salladsbädd

COCONUT TOSCA

In Sweden, tosca (croquant) is a favourite sweet topping for cakes and buns. This tray cake is delicious and easy to make!

200 g butter
4 eggs
500 ml sugar
300 ml flour
2 ½ tsp. baking powder
200 ml cocoa
2 tsp. vanilla sugar
pinch of salt

Tosca topping

100 g butter
250 ml sugar
100 ml pale syrup
150 ml cream
200 g coconut

Set the oven to 200 °C (fan-assisted), otherwise 225 °C. Melt the butter in a saucepan and whisk the eggs and sugar to make a batter.

Mix the flour, baking powder, cocoa, vanilla sugar and salt in a bowl. Pour the flour mixture into the batter and stir. Finally, pour in the melted butter and stir until you have mixed everything thoroughly. Pour the mixture into an oven tray lined with baking paper and bake at the centre of the oven for 10 minutes.

Make the tosca topping while the cake is in the oven. Melt the butter in a saucepan and mix in the sugar, syrup and cream, letting the mixture simmer for a few minutes. Stir in the coconut and bring to the boil again, stirring all the time.

Remove from the heat. Take the cake out of the oven and carefully pour the tosca over it. Bake for another 10 minutes or so until the tosca is golden.

Allow the cake to cool before cutting into even-sized pieces. Store the cakes in a tub in the refrigerator - they taste best chilled.

MAMA'S *sponge*

A classic sponge cake that you can turn into whatever you like! How about pear tosca, rhubarb or plum cake? I'm sure you can come up with loads of your favourite fruit and berry combos.

2 eggs
250 ml sugar
100 g butter
400 ml flour
2 tsp. baking powder
100 ml water

Set the oven to 175 °C (fan-assisted), otherwise 200 °C, and grease and crumb a cake tin. Whisk the eggs and sugar until fluffy. Melt the butter in a saucepan. Quickly stir the flour and baking powder into the egg mixture. Pour the water into the melted butter and then stir this into the mixture. Pour the finished cake batter into the tin. Bake the cake in the bottom half of the oven for 30-45 minutes.

Pear TOSCA

1 quantity sponge batter, see page 43
3-5 pears

Tosca topping

150 g butter
150 ml sugar
3 tbsp. cream
3 tbsp. flour
150 g roughly chopped almonds

Set the oven to 175 °C (fan-assisted), otherwise 200 °C. Make the mixture according to the recipe on page 43. Line the bottom of a spring form (approx. 30 cm in diameter) with a sheet of baking paper - you don't need to grease the sides. Pour the mixture into the tin. Cut each pear into roughly 8 wedges (there's no need to peel the pears). Tightly arrange the pear wedges on top of the mixture. Bake the cake in the bottom half of the oven for approximately 30 minutes.

Make the tosca topping while the cake is baking. Melt the butter in a saucepan and mix in the other ingredients. Simmer for 3 minutes, stirring all the time to prevent the mixture from burning at the bottom.

Take the cake out and carefully spread the tosca topping over it. Bake for a further 10 minutes or so until the tosca is nice and golden. Allow to cool a little before serving.

FRUIT *or* BERRY CAKE

1 quantity sponge batter, see page 43

fruit or berries, e.g. rhubarb, raspberries, apples or nectarines
150 ml crème fraîche
2 tsp. vanilla sugar
2 tbsp. sugar
juice of half a lemon, if desired

It's difficult to say how much fruit you need - it's a question of preference. I think it's nice to cover the entire cake. If you're using rhubarb, you need to cut it into pieces (around 1 cm is good). You can cut apples or nectarines into thin wedges or pieces - it doesn't matter - experiment!

Set the oven to 175 °C (fan-assisted), otherwise 200 °C, and make the mixture according to the recipe on page 43. Line the bottom of a spring form (approx. 30 cm in diameter) with a sheet of baking paper, but you don't need to grease the sides. Pour the mixture into the tin.

Mix your choice of fruit or berries with the crème fraiche, vanilla sugar and sugar. Spoon this mixture over the cake batter and sprinkle a tiny amount of sugar on top. Sometimes, I also squeeze over half a lemon.

Bake at the centre of the oven for approximately 30-40 minutes. Allow to cool slightly before serving.

PQRS

Banana cake

This banana cake is so delicious that even people who don't like bananas love it!

3-5 bananas
1 large egg
150 ml milk
100 ml crème fraîche
3 tbsp. rapeseed oil
350 ml all-purpose flour
200 ml sugar
2 tsp. baking powder
2 tsp. vanilla sugar
pinch of salt
butter, brown sugar and salt flakes for the cake tin

Set the oven to 175 °C (fan-assisted), otherwise 200 °C. Line the bottom of a spring form (approximately 24 cm in diameter) with a sheet of baking paper and grease it generously with the butter. 'Crumb' the tin with brown sugar and a scattering of salt flakes.

Peel the bananas and halve them lengthways. Place them cut-side down into the tin, covering the whole base with bananas.

Mix the egg, milk, crème fraîche and oil in a mixing bowl and all the dry ingredients in another. Fold the dry ingredients into the egg mixture and stir quickly to make a smooth batter. Pour the mixture over the bananas and bake at the centre of the oven for approximately 30-40 minutes. Allow the cake to cool a little before turning it upside down onto a dish - tap the bottom of the tin to loosen the bananas. Leave to cool completely and serve with lightly whipped cream.

Carrot CAKE

Virtually all cafés in Sweden now serve carrot cake – perhaps it's the easiest way of getting our kids to eat root vegetables? I've simplified the recipe to make it easier to memorise.

3 large carrots, grated (approx. 300 g)
3 eggs
300 ml sugar
300 ml flour
3 tsp. baking powder
33 ml rapeseed oil

Frosting

100 g Philadelphia cheese
60 g softened butter
400 ml icing sugar
grated zest of 2 limes

Set the oven to 175 °C (fan-assisted), otherwise 200 °C, and line the bottom of a spring form with a sheet of baking paper. You don't need to grease the sides.

Peel and grate the carrots. Whisk the egg and sugar until fluffy with an electric whisk. Stir in the flour and baking powder and then the carrots and oil, mixing to a smooth batter. Pour the mixture into the tin and bake in the bottom half of the oven for approximately 30 minutes. Allow the cake to cool before loosening from the tin.

Whisk the ingredients for the frosting with an electric whisk until smooth. Place the cake on a dish and spread the frosting over the cake.

If you prefer, you can make the cake a day in advance and prepare the frosting just before serving.

LEMON *and* LIME PIE

Serve this pie with lightly whipped cream and home-made raspberry jam – yum! Fresh strawberries are great too.

Pie crust

300 ml all-purpose flour
1 ½ tbsp. sugar
125 g butter
1 egg yolk

Filling

3 eggs
200 ml sugar
200 ml cream
2 tbsp. all-purpose flour
1 tsp. vanilla sugar
juice and grated zest of 1 lemon
juice and grated zest of 1 lime

Set the oven to 175 °C (fan-assisted), otherwise 200 °C. Line the bottom of a spring form with a sheet of baking paper. You don't need to grease the sides.

Put the flour, sugar and butter on your pastry board and chop it together with a knife - or you can pinch the mixture with your fingers to make a crumbly mass.

Mix the egg yolk in last and knead to form a small dough ball. Press the dough into the tin, pushing it up the sides a little to make a pastry shell. Whisk the eggs, sugar, cream, all-purpose flour and vanilla sugar in a mixing bowl. Thoroughly wash the lemon and lime and grate the zest. Squeeze the juice from both fruits and add with the zest to the mixture.

Pour the mixture into the pastry shell and cover with a lid or some foil. Bake in the centre of the oven for 30 minutes. Remove the lid/foil and leave the pie in the oven for a few more minutes to brown a little. Allow to cool before removing from the tin, and serve with lightly whipped cream and raspberry jam or fresh berries.

FAVORITE
cheesecake

Base

12 digestive biscuits
75 g melted butter
2 tbsp. sugar
1 egg

Filling

450 g Philadelphia cheese
250 ml sugar
1 tsp. vanilla sugar
3 eggs
grated zest of 1 lemon
450 ml crème fraîche
200-300 ml raspberry jam

Crumble the biscuits - I usually put them in a mixing bowl and crush them with a pestle. You can whizz them in a mixer, if you prefer.

Melt the butter. Pour the sugar and melted butter into the biscuit crumbs and stir (continue with the mixer, if using). Mix in the egg.

Line the bottom of a spring form with a sheet of baking paper. You don't need to grease the sides. Press the crumb mixture into the tin, pushing it up the sides a little. Refrigerate the crumb mixture while you make the filling. Set the oven to 160 °C (fan-assisted), otherwise 185 °C.

Whisk the Philadelphia smooth with an electric whisk, pouring in the sugar and vanilla sugar while you do so.

Mix in one egg at a time and continue whisking until everything is well mixed. Wash the lemon thoroughly and grate the zest. Add the lemon zest to the mixture, and quickly stir in the crème fraîche. Pour the filling into the tin and bake at the bottom of the oven for 50-60 minutes. The cake should be a bit wobbly when you take it out - it will firm up as it cools.

Once completely cool, spread a nice even layer of raspberry jams over the top.

PRUNE PIE

This pie is very special to me. All my aunties baked it, just like my mum. When I was a child, I liked it best when it came straight out of the freezer. My recipe has lemon in it to add a little acidic contrast to the sweetness.

Filling

250 g prunes
50-100 ml sugar
just under 100 ml water
2 tbsp. potato flour
dissolved in 50 ml water

Pastry

450 ml flour
1 ½ tsp. baking powder
just over 100 ml sugar
125 g butter
just under 100 ml milk
1 beaten egg
1 tbsp. cream

Boil the prunes, sugar and water on a low heat for approximately 30 minutes. Squeeze in a little lemon and thicken the prune mixture with the potato flour and water to make a really thick cream. Allow to cool.

Set the oven to 200 °C (fan-assisted), otherwise 225 °C. Mix the flour, baking powder and sugar in a mixing bowl. Cut the butter into small pieces. Pinch the butter into the flour mixture and then add the milk. Work to a dough. Scoop it out to knead on the work surface, if necessary.

Divide the dough in two pieces, one slightly larger than the other. Roll them both out and put the larger one in a rectangular oven dish (approx. 30 X 20 cm) with baking paper at the bottom. The pastry should cover the whole base of the dish, and can even hang out a little over the sides. Pour the cooled prune cream into the pie shell and cover with the smaller piece of pastry. Fold the overhanging pastry edges on top to 'seal' the pie. Prick the pastry lid with a fork. Whisk the egg and cream and brush the pie with the mixture. Bake at the centre of the oven for approximately 30 minutes.

Allow the pie to cool before cutting into pieces. Serve with cream or try eating it semi-frozen!

Pssst !!!
Du vet väl om att du kan köpa frysta bullar o bröd.
5st kanel el kardemummabulla
6st morotsbullar
6st rågkringlor
50:-/påse

kaka på kaka på kaka på kaka på kaka på kaka
STARTA DAGEN
PÅ
kaka på kaka
Nyhet GRÖT
Havregrynsgröt med
spännande tillbehör!
Tex. "Härgjord" sylt torkad
frukt jordnötssmör bär mm......
skapa din egen favorit
KAKAS FRUKOSTPAKET
kaffe
morotsfralla
yoghurt med
hărgjord granola

BANANA *cake* WITH PALE CHOCOLATE FROSTING

I think the frosting on this cake should be really pale, like milk chocolate. If you like it darker, just add more cocoa!

150 ml sugar
3 tbsp. softened butter
1 ½ tbsp. rapeseed oil
2 eggs
400 ml flour
2 tsp. baking powder
2 tsp. vanilla sugar
pinch of salt
4 bananas
50 ml milk

Frosting

100 g Philadelphia cheese
60 g butter
400 ml icing sugar
approx. 1 tsp. cocoa (or according to taste)

blueberries to garnish

Set the oven to 175 °C (fan-assisted), otherwise 200 °C. Line the bottom of a spring form (approximately 24 cm in diameter) with a sheet of baking paper.

Mix the sugar, butter and oil together before stirring in one egg at a time and then mixing in the dry ingredients. Mash the banana with the milk in a bowl, and add to your mixture. There's no need to stir too much.

Pour the batter into the tin and bake the cake at the centre of the oven for approximately 40 minutes. The cake should rise in the middle. Allow to cool in the tin before turning out onto a dish. Mix the ingredients for the frosting with an electric whisk and beat until completely smooth. Spread the frosting over the cake and garnish with blueberries.

ALMOND
cake

This is my daughter Clara's show-stopper – and a given on the menu when she helps out at the café.

5 egg whites
200 ml sugar
150 g grated almonds

Butter cream

175 g softened butter
5 egg yolks
150 ml sugar
150 ml cream
pinch of salt
1-2 tsp. vanilla sugar
approx. 150 ml flaked almonds

Set the oven to 170 °C (fan-assisted), otherwise 195 °C. Whisk the egg whites until stiff in a clean, dry stainless steel bowl. If you have to make do with a plastic one, give it an extra wipe with a clean, dry tea towel to remove any grease.

Add the sugar a little at a time and whisk until you have a nice, firm meringue batter. Grate the almonds in a nut grinder and fold them into the mixture with a spatula.

Spread the mixture to make two round meringue bases, each measuring approximately 30 cm in diameter. Make each one on separate sheets of baking paper. Bake at the centre of the oven for 20 minutes until the bases are a nice colour. You can bake both at the same time in a fan-assisted oven, otherwise bake each one separately. Cube the butter and place on a dish. Mix the egg yolks, sugar and cream in a thick-bottomed saucepan. Put the pan on a medium to high heat and start whisking, continuing until the cream has thickened. Remove the saucepan from the heat and continue to whisk while you add the butter, a little at a time. Whisk until the butter has completely melted. Add salt and vanilla sugar and allow the cream to cool.

Remove the meringue bases from the baking paper and spread half the butter cream on one. Sandwich together with the other base and spread the remaining cream on top.

Lightly toast the flaked almonds in a dry, non-stick pan. Sprinkle the toasted almonds over the cake and leave in a cool place until it is time to serve. Chilled whipped cream is delicious with this!

French CHOCOLATE CAKE

This delicious chocolate cake is inspired by the one served at the Rosendal café in Stockholm, but we've tweaked the recipe here and there to create our own. It's a rich, wonderfully chocolaty cake and the use of good quality cocoa is important. Choose your favourite cocoa and adjust the amount to suit you. Wrapped in aluminium foil, this cake will keep fresh for a week.

200 g butter
4 eggs
550 ml sugar
4 tsp. vanilla sugar
400 ml cocoa
300 ml all-purpose flour
pinch of salt flakes

Ganache

100 g dark chocolate
100 ml whipping cream

Set the oven to 175 °C (fan-assisted), otherwise 200 °C. Line the bottom of a spring form with a sheet of baking paper - you don't need to grease the sides. Melt the butter. Whisk the eggs and sugar in a mixing bowl. Stir in the dry ingredients and finally, the slightly cooled butter.

Spread the mixture over the base of the tin and bake at the centre the oven for approximately 15 minutes. Take out the cake and leave to cool.

Meanwhile, make the ganache. Finely chop the chocolate. Heat the cream in a saucepan, remove the saucepan from the heat and add the chopped chocolate. Stir until the chocolate has fully melted. Spread the ganache over the cake and leave to set. Serve small slices of the cake with lightly whipped cream, if desired.

Basic
BUN *dough*

You can make lots of delicious things with this basic sweet dough recipe.

Makes 20-25 buns

1 pkt. yeast for sweet dough
175 g butter
500 ml milk
pinch of salt
150 ml sugar
approx. 1400 ml all-purpose flour

Crumble the yeast in the bowl of your mixer, if using. Melt the butter in a saucepan, switch off the heat and pour in the milk. Check the temperature with a thermometer or do the finger test - the liquid should be max 37 °C. Pour a little of the dough liquid onto the yeast and stir until the yeast has dissolved. Now add the rest of the dough liquid, along with the salt, sugar and half of the flour.

Work in the rest of the flour, a little at a time, until the dough loosens slightly from the sides of the bowl. I usually work the dough for 5 minutes in the machine, but it will take longer by hand. Dust your fingers with flour and check the consistency of the dough - it shouldn't stick to your finger but almost.

Detach your bowl, sprinkle the insides with a little flour and cover with a clean tea towel. Leave to prove for approximately 30 minutes.

Cinnamon BUNS
and more

1 quantity of dough according to
the recipe on p. 69

Filling

250 g butter, softened
200-250 ml caster sugar
vanilla sugar according to taste
cinnamon, freshly ground cardamom
or raisins

or:
250 ml crème fraîche
2 tbsp. vanilla sugar

Brush and garnish with:

1 beaten egg
pearl sugar

Scoop the dough onto a lightly floured surface. Roll the dough with a light hand, gently pressing outwards to form a rectangle. If you don't have much space, split the dough in two and make two batches. Spread on the butter and sprinkle over the sugar.

Now decide how to flavour the buns - I always use vanilla sugar, then sprinkle on cinnamon, freshly ground cardamom or raisins. Sometimes, I mix crème fraîche with vanilla sugar, spread this thinly over the dough and sprinkle over raisins - it's really delicious. Try out your own combinations! Roll up the rectangle lengthways to make a long snake, and position it seam-side down. Cut the snake into evenly sized pieces and place cut-side up into bun cases on an oven tray. Leave to prove under a proving cloth for 30 minutes. Set the oven to 200 °C (fan-assisted), otherwise 225 °C.

Brush the buns with beaten egg and sprinkle over pearl sugar. Bake in the centre of the oven for approximately 10-15 minutes.

kaka

Butter cake or wreath

Make the dough as previously described but instead of putting the buns in cases, place them together in a greased spring form to make 'butter cake'. Be careful not to squash them together too much. Leave to prove in the tin under a tea towel for approximately 30 minutes. Set the oven to 175 °C (fan-assisted), otherwise 200 °C. Bake in the lower half of the oven for approximately 30 minutes.

Or...

Roll out, fill, and roll up the dough. Place 'the snake' on a sheet of baking paper on an oven tray, joining both ends of the snake to make a wreath. To create the plait effect, use scissors to slash half way through the dough and fold each cut piece alternately right and left (see picture). Leave to prove on the tray under a tea towel for approximately 30 minutes. Set the oven to 185 °C (fan-assisted), otherwise 210 °C, and bake in the bottom half of the oven for approximately 30 minutes.

FOCACCIA

This bread is fabulous with soup or salad. To achieve the chewy consistency of focaccia, the dough has relatively little flour in it and has to be kneaded for quite a while, so use a machine if possible. Experiment with toppings to suit you!

Makes 1 focaccia

50 g yeast
500 ml lukewarm water
1 tbsp. salt
100 ml sesame seeds
1 L durum wheat flour
100 ml olive oil
50 ml oil
black olives
2 tbsp. dried rosemary
salt flakes

Crumble the yeast in a mixing bowl and pour in the water. Mix until the yeast has dissolved. Add the salt and sesame seeds and stir in half of the flour. Add the oil, and then work in the rest of the flour. Work the dough in your machine for around 10 minutes. Leave to prove under a tea towel for about 30 minutes before rolling out.

Oil an oven tray or large oven dish and scoop the dough onto it. Flatten the bread with your hands until it is approximately 1 cm thick. Use your fingers to press a few holes into the dough and leave to prove under a clean tea towel for approximately 30 minutes. Set the oven to 200 °C (fan-assisted), otherwise 225 °C.

Drizzle a little oil over the bread and sprinkle on olives, rosemary and salt flakes. Bake in the bottom half of the oven for approximately 30 minutes.

Tip!

Experiment with different toppings for the focaccia. For example, sliced red onion or sun-dried tomatoes are delicious!

CARROT
bread rolls

These soft moist rolls have become a classic at our café, Kaka på Kaka. Fill them with cheese, ham, Dijon mustard, salad and tomatoes for a deliciously filling lunch sandwich!

Makes approx. 16 rolls

50 g butter
500 ml milk
50 g yeast
3 tbsp. dark syrup (or treacle/dark molasses)
1 tbsp. salt
700 ml sifted rye flour
500 g grated carrots
700 ml all-purpose flour
beaten egg
pumpkin seeds

Melt the butter in a saucepan and pour in the milk. Heat to 37 °C - you can use a thermometer or test with your finger. Crumble the yeast into the bowl of your mixer and pour on the liquid, stirring until the yeast has dissolved. Pour in the syrup (molasses) and salt and mix in the rye flour. Leave the machine to work the dough for a while. Grate the carrots and mix them into the dough. Add almost all the flour, a little at a time, and continue working the dough in the mixer for approximately 5-10 minutes. If the dough feels too sticky, you can add a little more flour but it mustn't get dry. Powder a little flour around the dough and leave to prove under a tea towel for 30-40 minutes. Set the oven to 200 °C (fan-assisted), otherwise 225 °C.

Tip the dough onto a floured surface and divide into two lengths with a spatula. Divide each length into 7-8 pieces and put the pieces cut-side up on an oven tray lined with baking paper. Leave to prove for a further 30 minutes under a tea towel.

Brush with beaten egg and sprinkle over the pumpkin seeds. Bake at the centre of the oven for approximately 15 minutes. Allow to cool on a rack, under a tea towel.

Bread in a jar!

Mix all the dry ingredients in a jar and write a note with things that need to be added. Makes a lovely present!

KAKA PÅ KAKA'S
rustic loaf

This bread contains quite a lot of different ingredients, so while I'm making it, I prepare several batches of the dry ingredients and put them in plastic bags. When I get round to baking again, all I need to do is add the sour milk and carrots.

2 loaves

500 ml all-purpose flour
400 ml rolled oats
250 ml sifted rye flour
250 ml wholemeal flour
100 ml whole or crushed linseeds
100 ml sesame seeds
100 ml pumpkin seeds
100 ml sunflower seeds
1 tbsp. salt
4 tsp. bicarbonate of soda
1 L sour milk
2 large grated carrots
butter and rolled oats for the bread tins

Set the oven to 190 °C (fan-assisted), otherwise 215 °C. Grease two bread tins and crumb with rolled oats.

Thoroughly mix the dry ingredients in a mixing bowl (or bags or jars if you're preparing a bread mix to save for later). Next, stir the sour milk and carrots into the bowl and pour the batter into the tins. Sprinkle on your choice of seeds and bake at the centre of the oven for approximately 90 minutes.

Tip the bread straight out onto a rack and allow to cool without covering. Store the loaves covered with a tea towel, and once you've started cutting one, keep it cut-side down on a plate (not in a plastic bag) to preserve the delicious crust. The bread will keep fresh for several days.

RYE RINGS

These wonderfully chewy bread rings are perfect filled with smoked salmon, cream cheese and salad - a bit like bagels! Alternatively, try spreading on mayo, salad, a fried egg and tomato or toast the bread and top with cheese and marmalade.

Makes 12-16

50 g yeast
600 ml warm water (37 °C)
2 tbsp. dark syrup (or treacle/dark molasses)
1 tbsp. salt
700 ml sifted rye flour
250 ml rolled oats
1 egg
500 ml all-purpose flour

Crumble the yeast in the bowl of your mixer. Pour the water over the yeast and stir until the yeast has dissolved. Add the syrup and salt and mix in the sifted rye flour, rolled oats and egg. Finally, work in the flour a little at a time. Work the dough in the machine for approximately 5 minutes. Since the dough is quite sticky and difficult to combine, a dough hook is really handy here. Sprinkle some flour around the dough and leave to prove for 30 minutes.

Set the oven to 185 °C (fan-assisted), otherwise 210 °C. Tip the dough out onto a floured surface. Divide into 12-16 pieces and shape each one in your hands to make a flat bun measuring approximately 10 cm in diameter. Pinch a hole in the middle of each bun with your thumb and forefinger and arrange them side by side on an oven tray lined with baking paper. Leave to prove under a tea towel for 30 minutes. Bake at the centre of the oven for approximately 10-15 minutes until lightly golden.

Päron-
marmelad

JAM

This is embarrassingly easy! I always make fairly small batches of jam so that I can use less sugar (most jams need a lot of sugar to preserve them for longer). The result is a much tastier jam and I use it all up before it has a chance to go mouldy. I love making nectarine marmalade, but you can concoct your own favourites!

500 g fruit or berries,
fresh or frozen (defrosted)
approx. 200 ml jam sugar, more if
the berries/fruit are acidic

optional: boil with a vanilla or
cinnamon stick

Rinse the fruit or berries. Peel and core the fruit and cut into pieces. I often don't bother with peeling if the fruit is organic and skins are in good condition. Put the berries or fruit in a thick-bottomed saucepan and mix in the jam sugar. Stir on a low heat to dissolve the sugar, and allow to boil for at least 5 minutes or until the fruit/berries are reasonably soft. Keep stirring as you do this.

Pour the jam into clean jars and store in the refrigerator. The jam will keep for about a month - just check its appearance, taste and smell!

Tip!

Add a few drops of lemon to the warm jam for more acidity.

PICKLED
red onion and fennel

A tasty accompaniment for hamburgers, pulled pork or salads. The recipe uses '1-2-3' proportions for the pickling liquid and you can put whatever you like in it – experiment!

100 ml distilled white vinegar (12 %)
200 ml sugar
300 ml water

To pickle: 2-3 red onions
or 1 large fennel

Mix the vinegar, sugar and water in a saucepan and bring to the boil. Remove from the heat and stir until the sugar has melted.

Thinly slice the red onion or fennel. Place in a jar and pour on the slightly cooled pickling liquid. Screw on the lid and leave to cool completely before storing in the refrigerator. The pickle will keep for at least a week.

PESTO

50 g fresh basil
1 clove of garlic
pinch of salt
100 ml pine nuts
approx. 250 ml grated parmesan
200 ml olive oil

Whizz the basil, garlic, salt and pine nuts in a mixer to make a smooth paste. Add the grated parmesan and drizzle in the oil, a little at a time, mixing everything thoroughly. Store in a sealed jar in the refrigerator. Pouring a little extra oil on top of the pesto in the jar helps it keep fresh for longer.

Use the pesto...

with freshly made pasta, soups, as a salad dressing or on toasted sandwiches with tomato and mozzarella.

havregryn solrosfrö sesam
linfrö pumpafrö russin
aprikos
Granola
rapsolja
tranbär cocosflingor
ingefära appeljuice honung
kanel kärlek

GRANOLA

Granola is great to make at home because you can add all your favourite ingredients. Here's my version.

1 litre rolled oats

100 ml each of:
linseed
sesame seeds
pumpkin seeds
sunflower seeds
1 tbsp. cinnamon or crushed cardamom
just under 100 ml rapeseed oil
50 ml honey
100 ml concentrated apple juice
200 ml coconut flakes

Additionally, a handful of:
raisins
dried cranberries
dried ginger
dried figs
dried apricots

Set the oven to 200 °C (fan-assisted), otherwise 225 °C. Pour the rolled oats, linseed, sesame seeds, pumpkin seeds and sunflower seeds into an oven tray lined with baking paper. Sprinkle over cinnamon or cardamom, drizzle over the oil and honey and pour on the concentrated apple juice. Mix everything together and roast at the centre of the oven until golden (approximately 15-20 minutes). Monitor this carefully and stir the mixture occasionally so that the granola browns evenly and does not burn. Remove the tray from the oven and allow to cool.

Lightly toast the coconut flakes in a dry pan. Chop the dried fruit and berries and add them with the coconut flakes to the granola once completely cool. Store in a sealed jar. This is a really luxurious topping for your breakfast yoghurt or porridge!

PIMP
your porridge!

Oatmeal porridge – a simple and delicious Swedish classic. Use your favourite brand of oats and why not add a knob of butter occasionally for a real treat? Go wild with the toppings, of course!

You might like to try these toppings:
jam
peanut butter
honey
cinnamon
dried or fresh fruit
fresh berries

Mix 100 ml rolled oats and 200 ml water in a saucepan. Add salt and allow to boil for a few minutes until the porridge is nice and thick, stirring occasionally. Plate up the porridge and pimp with your favourite toppings!

TOMATO SAUCE

You can vary and add to this tomato sauce as much as you like. Have it with pasta or as a BBQ accompaniment, or blend and dilute to make a soup, as on page 102. Use fresh or tinned tomatoes, but if you're using fresh ones, roast them in the oven first for the best flavour. And the better the tomatoes, the better the finished result!

Serves 4

2 cans of tomatoes (preferably organic plum tomatoes)
or 1 kg fresh tomatoes
1 onion
1 clove of garlic
4 tbsp. good olive oil
200 ml water
1 vegetable stock cube
salt flakes and pepper
optional pinch of sugar
1 pot of fresh basil

If using fresh tomatoes, you also need:
50 ml olive oil
salt flakes
dried rosemary
2-3 cloves of garlic

Preparing fresh tomatoes:

Set the oven to 225 °C (fan-assisted), otherwise 250 °C. Cut the tomatoes into pieces and arrange on an oven tray lined with baking paper. Drizzle over 50 ml olive oil and mix with salt flakes, rosemary and 2-3 cloves of garlic. Roast at the centre of the oven for approximately 30 minutes until the tomatoes have browned a little.

Peel and chop the onion and garlic. Sauté them in the oil in a pan, being careful not to burn the garlic and make it bitter. Pour on the tomatoes - if using tinned ones, crush them a little with a fork or cut with scissors. Add the water and crumble in the stock cube. Add salt and pepper and simmer on a low heat for as long as you have time. You can remove the pan from the heat after 15 minutes but the longer you leave it, the better. I often let mine simmer for hours.

Taste and adjust with a pinch of sugar, stock or salt, if necessary. Finally, cut the basil and serve with the sauce, grated parmesan and your favourite pasta or make the soup on page 102.

Vary your tomato sauce!

Cut mozzarella into small pieces and mix with the pasta and tomato sauce. Serve immediately.

Add olives and chilli for a little more sting.

Add wine instead of water.

Fry some bacon or pieces of chicken and mix into the sauce.

Fry minced beef and add to the sauce to make bolognaise.

Use the tomato sauce on pizza.

The sauce is ideal for freezing - handy when you need to get dinner ready in a hurry!

TOMATO SOUP
with dumplings
AND BASIL OIL

A versatile soup you can get creative with.

Serves 4

1 quantity tomato sauce, see page 97

pinch of chilli flakes
100 ml whipping cream

Dumplings

200 g flour
3 egg yolks
225 g cream cheese (e.g. ricotta or Philadelphia)
30 g grated parmesan
salt
a drizzle of oil

Soup
Make the tomato sauce according to the basic recipe on page 97. Add a pinch of chilli flakes to lend some comforting heat to the soup. Blend directly in the pot with a hand mixer and pour in the cream. Mix a little more, and then it's ready!

Basil oil

Blend 100 ml oil, ½ a pot of fresh basil and a pinch of salt. Serve the piping hot soup with the dumplings and drizzle over the basil oil.

Dumplings
Mix the ingredients together to make a slightly sticky dough. Roll out a finger-thick snake onto a floured surface and cut in pieces approximately 4 cm wide. Press each one down a little with a fork, if you like. Bring water to the boil in a saucepan - it's good to have one that contains at least 2 litres. Add salt. Drop the dumplings into the boiling water. You may have to make two batches, depending on the size of your pan. Boil the dumplings until they float up and remove them with a slotted spoon. Put them in a bowl and drizzle over a little oil to prevent them from sticking together.

CAULIFLOWER *soup* *with a* STING

This soup is smooth and creamy but full of character from the lemon and chilli.

Serves 4

1 large head of cauliflower
2-3 shallots
1 generous tbsp. butter
500-600 ml water
½ tsp. chilli flakes
1-2 vegetable stock cubes
300 ml crème fraîche
200 ml milk
juice of 1 lime or lemon
salt
freshly ground black pepper

Separate the head of cauliflower into small florets. Peel the onion and cut into small pieces. Sauté in the butter in a large saucepan. Add almost all of the cauliflower, saving a few florets for garnish.

Pour on the water, add the chilli flakes and crumble in a stock cube. Allow to simmer until the cauliflower is soft, for approximately 15 minutes. Blend the soup and add the crème fraîche and milk. Squeeze in the lemon or lime juice and season with salt, pepper and more stock, if desired.

Garnish:

a few cauliflower florets
2tbsp. rapeseed oil
sesame seeds
chilli flakes to taste

Set the oven to 225 °C (fan-assisted), otherwise 250 °C. Arrange the cauliflower florets you have saved on an oven tray.

Drizzle over the rapeseed oil and sprinkle on some sesame seeds, along with some chilli flakes, if desired. Roast in the centre of the oven until the cauliflower is slightly golden. Serve the soup garnished with the roasted cauliflower.

Tip!

You can also use sausage or crispy bacon as a topping for the soup.

GREEN
pea soup
or CRÈME NINON

A super quick and easy lunch, appetizer or supper!

Serves 4

1 kg frozen green peas
700 ml water
1 tbsp. or 1 cube of good vegetable stock
100-200 ml crème fraîche or cream
salt and freshly ground black pepper

Bring the peas, water and stock to the boil in a saucepan. Blend thoroughly, add crème fraîche or cream, and blend a little more. Season with salt and pepper and serve with a dollop of crème fraîche. You can top the soup with oven roasted air-dried ham for an extra special twist.

Tip!

Mix crumbled goat's cheese with a little Greek yoghurt and spread on a piece of toast. Delicious with the soup!

CARROT SOUP

Serves 4

just over 1 kg carrots
approx. 1 litre water
1 vegetable stock cube
pinch of chilli powder
250 ml crème fraîche
a few drops of lemon to taste
salt and pepper

Topping

1 carrot
1 parsnip
2 tbsp. oil
salt
crème fraîche

Start with the topping. Set the oven to 225 °C (fan-assisted), otherwise 250 °C. Peel the carrot and parsnip and thinly shred. Spread the vegetable shreds over an oven tray lined with baking paper. Drizzle over the oil and add salt. Roast in the oven for a few minutes until nice and golden.

Peel the carrots for the soup and cut into pieces. Place them in a pot and pour on the water to scarcely cover the carrots. Add the stock cube and chilli powder, bring to the boil and simmer until the carrots are soft. Blend the soup smooth, spoon in the crème fraîche and blend a little more. Season with a few drops of lemon and salt and pepper.

Top the soup with a dollop of crème fraîche and the roasted root vegetable shreds.

TUSCAN
bean soup

Serves 4-6

3 carrots
2 onions
1 small leek
3 sticks of celery
1 small red chilli
½ savoy cabbage
50 ml olive oil
½ tsp. rosemary
½ tsp. thyme
1.3-1.5 L water
2 vegetable stock cubes
1 can white beans
1 can kidney beans
2 fresh tomatoes
or 10 cherry tomatoes
approx. 100 g fresh baby spinach

Garnish: parmesan and fresh thyme

Peel the carrots and onions, and cut into fairly small pieces. Cut the leek lengthways and rinse thoroughly. Chop the leek, celery and chilli into small pieces. Shred the savoy cabbage. Sauté everything in the oil in a large pot with the herbs. Pour on the water and crumble in the stock cubes. Simmer on a medium heat for approximately 10 minutes.

Drain and rinse the beans in a colander. Add the beans to the soup and simmer for a further 5 minutes. Cut the tomatoes into medium sized pieces and add them last, with the spinach. Stir and serve with parmesan shavings and fresh thyme.

Serve with focaccia!

Focaccia garnished with red onion, rosemary and salt flakes is delicious with this soup (see page 76 for recipe).

IKEA
172 78
40

VEGETABLE *gratin*

... HEAVENLY *and moreish*

I always roast the vegetables in the oven for a while before putting them in the oven dish. It gives them a tender, sweeter flavour.

Serves 4

4 potatoes
½ aubergine
20 button mushrooms
3 carrots
2 parsnips
2 red peppers
1 leek
olive oil
salt
1 bag of fresh leaf spinach (65 g)
250 ml crème fraîche
200 ml cream
400 ml grated cheese (cheddar and mozzarella are tasty)

Set the oven to 200 °C (fan-assisted), otherwise 225 °C. Slice all the vegetables but reserve the bag of spinach and put the sliced potatoes to one side. Arrange the other vegetables on oven trays lined with baking paper. I usually separate each type of vegetable so that if one is ready before the other I can simply take it out and let the rest continue cooking. Drizzle over olive oil and add salt. Roast the vegetables in the middle of the oven until nicely coloured, for around 10-20 minutes.

Boil the sliced potatoes in salted water for approximately 5 minutes. Pour off the water and leave the potatoes to steam off a little. Grease a gratin dish and arrange the potato slices at the bottom. Add half of the cheese and then half the bag of spinach. Continue layering with the roasted vegetables, then the rest of the spinach, and finally a layer of potato and the remaining cheese. Whisk the crème fraîche and cream and pour over the gratin. Bake in the bottom half of the oven for approximately 30 minutes, sprinkling on a little extra cheese in the last 10 minutes, if you wish.

Serve the vegetable gratin with a green salad, French dressing and toasted seeds, or as a meat accompaniment.

STUFFED tomatoes

If you have any cooked rice left over, this is the perfect way to use it. Otherwise, boil fresh rice and cool before mixing with the filling. I like jasmine rice but short grain works well too. Aubergine, courgette, mushrooms, leek or bell peppers are delicious choices for the filling. Serve with a nice salad or as a meat accompaniment.

For each portion:

2 tomatoes
4 button mushrooms and/or your preferred vegetables
oil for frying
2 tbsp. grated cheese, e.g. cheddar
approx. 200 ml cold boiled rice
1 tbsp. pesto
2 slices mozzarella
salt and pepper

Set the oven to 225 °C (fan-assisted), otherwise 250 °C. Cut out 'lids' from the tomatoes and carefully scoop out the tomato flesh with a spoon. Fry the mushrooms in a little oil and grate the cheese. Mix the mushrooms, cheese, rice and pesto and season with salt and pepper. Stuff the tomatoes with the mixture and put a slice of mozzarella on each tomato before topping with the 'lid'. Arrange the tomatoes on an oven tray lined with baking paper, packing them tightly so that they support each other. Bake at the centre of the oven for approximately 30 minutes.

Halloumi BURGERS

You can serve these burgers with mashed potato, potato wedges, rice or salad, or why not have them as a snack?

Serves 4

4 carrots
2 parsnips
1 aubergine
1 large leek
200 g mushrooms
150 g halloumi
1 egg
2 tbsp. flour
salt and pepper

Set the oven to 225 °C (fan-assisted), otherwise 250 °C. Roughly grate the carrot, parsnip and aubergine. Cut the leek lengthways and rinse thoroughly. Chop the mushrooms and leek and pile into an oven tray. Drizzle over olive oil and roast in the oven for approximately 15 minutes. Remove and allow to cool. Transfer the roasted vegetables to a mixing bowl.

Grate the halloumi and mix it in with the egg. Sprinkle over flour, add salt and pepper and mix together. Heat a frying pan with a little oil. Shape the mixture into round burgers - you can flatten them with a spatula in the pan. Fry the burgers on a medium high heat. Try not to turn them too soon - it's easier to prevent them from falling apart once the egg has coagulated and the cheese has melted a little. Three to four minutes on each side usually does the trick.

PRAWN SALAD
Swedish style

A delicious, refreshing, satisfying salad – best made with fresh prawns that you peel at home.

For each portion:

approx. 150 ml cooked whole grains, e.g. bulgur, pearl barley, kamut
approx. 100 g peeled prawns
piece of cucumber
½ avocado
1 tomato or a few small ones in different colours
2 cauliflower florets
handful of mixed salad leaves

Dressing (per portion):

1-2 tbsp. mayonnaise
1 tsp. horseradish
1-2 tsp. water

Boil the grains according to the instructions and leave to cool. Peel the prawns. Peel and core the cucumber and cut into half-moons. Cut the avocado and tomatoes into wedges and divide the cauliflower into small florets. Put the salad leaves on plates and arrange the grains and vegetables on top. Add the prawns. Mix the dressing and drizzle over the salad. Serve with a lemon wedge, sprig of dill and some good bread.

... *and*

ASIAN STYLE

For each portion:

150 ml cooked pearl couscous
50 ml frozen soya beans
100 g peeled prawns
piece of cucumber
a few thin slices of fennel
a small piece of black radish
handful of mixed salad leaves
1/4 courgette

Dressing (per portion):

25 ml lime juice
½ tbsp. runny honey
just over ½ tsp. sesame oil
¼ finely chopped red chilli
approx. 1 tsp. sesame seeds, black and white if possible
salt

Boil the couscous and leave to cool. Defrost the soya beans - just rinse them in lukewarm water. Peel the prawns. Peel and core the cucumber and cut into half-moons. Thinly slice the fennel and cut the radish into thin batons. Make shavings of the courgette. Put the salad leaves on plates and arrange the couscous and vegetables on top. Whisk the dressing together and mix a little of it with the prawns. Put the prawns on the salad and sprinkle over some extra sesame seeds. Serve with a wedge of lime, the rest of the dressing and some nice bread.

SALAD *with chèvre* and pan-fried *plums*

I usually assemble this salad straight onto the plate. I haven't given exact amounts – you can adjust them to suit you. Serve as a starter or main course.

For each portion:

100 ml cooked pearl couscous
generous handful of mixed salad leaves
piece of courgette
piece of cucumber
1 slice of chèvre
2-3 plums (or 1 nectarine)
1 tbsp. butter
2 tsp. honey
2 tsp. crema balsamico
a little water
toasted sunflower and pumpkin seeds
salt and pepper

Boil the couscous and leave to cool. Mix the different salad leaves in a large bowl. I usually have iceberg or romaine lettuce as a base and mix in a few different kinds of smaller leaves. Put the salad on plates and sprinkle over the pearl couscous. Shave the courgette thinly. Cut the cucumber lengthways, core and cut into half-moons. Distribute the courgette and cucumber over the couscous and add a slice of chèvre to each plate.

Halve the plums or nectarines and remove the stones. Fry the fruit halves in a little butter in a frying pan and drizzle over a few drops of honey. The fruit is done once it has browned a little. Add salt and pepper. Arrange the fried plums on top of the goats' cheese, drizzle over crema balsamico (dilute with a little water, if you like) and sprinkle on some toasted sunflower and pumpkin seeds.

Tip!

Nectarines or peaches make good substitutes for plums, if you can't get them.

Cauliflower *salad*

Serve this salad as an accompaniment to meat or fish or with a tomato and leaf salad. You can prepare the cauliflower salad in advance.

Serves 4–6

1 head of cauliflower
2 large bunches of dill
50 ml capers
salt and pepper
sunflower seeds to taste

Dressing

3 tbsp. Skåne mustard
or other coarse grained mustard
2 tbsp. Dijon mustard
3 tbsp. honey
3 tbsp. white wine vinegar
3 tbsp. olive oil

Whisk together the ingredients for the dressing. Separate the cauliflower into small florets and mix with the dressing. Leave to absorb for at least 30 minutes. Pluck off the dill fronds and roughly chop. Mix the dill and capers with the cauliflower and season with salt and pepper. Sprinkle over some sunflower seeds, if desired.

Assistent

Index

kaka på kaka
Lunch
ONSDAG • Sallad m. getost päron & balsamicovinegrätt
TORSDAG • Paj m. spenat feta & tomat
Blekingesparris
från Listerlandet
Kl. 1
Ekologiskt odlade